Living and Learning in

MW01490814

Elsi Dodge
elsidodge@aol.com

Cathy Howe
cathy@bvchristian.org

Living and Learning in God's World is published by Steuben Press, Centennial, Colorado. No portion of this book may be reproduced without the express written consent of Steuben Press, Elsi Dodge or Cathy Howe.

Living and Learning in God's World is written by Elsi Dodge
Copyright 2010 © Elsi Dodge and Cathy Howe

Unless otherwise indicated, all Scripture is taken from the Holy Bible, NEW INTERNATIONAL READER'S VERSION®. Copyright © 1996, 1998 International Bible Society. All rights reserved throughout the world. Used by permission of International Bible Society.

All photographs Copyright © 2010, Elsi Dodge. Photographs taken by Elsi Dodge, Jessica Ogden, and Stan Silverman.

Published and Printed by:
    Steuben Press
    an Imprint of R&R Graphics, Inc.
    4901 E. Dry Creek Rd., #160
    Centennial, CO 80122

Printed in the United States of America

I.S.B.N. 978-1-935787-12-9

This book is dedicated, with love and gratitude to God:

For you created my inmost being;
you knit me together in my mother's womb.
I praise you because I am fearfully and wonderfully made;
your works are wonderful, I know that full well.
My frame was not hidden from you
when I was made in the secret place.
When I was woven together in the depths of the earth,
your eyes saw my unformed body.
All the days ordained for me were written in your book
before one of them came to be.

How precious to me are your thoughts, O God!
How vast is the sum of them!
Were I to count them, they would outnumber the grains of sand.
When I awake, I am still with you.
(Psalm 139:13-18)

• Note: (Genesis 1:1) means the words are a quotation from the NIrV version of the Bible. (see Genesis 1:1) means the words are a paraphrase, that the authors have told the sense of the passage in their own words.

Words in the Bible

Words are important to God! In the Bible, God used words when He talked to people. One time, God's people could tell if someone was a friend or an enemy, just by listening to how that person pronounced a word. (see Judges 12)

The words Jesus spoke are so important that many Bibles print them in red, so they're easy to find.

And, when Jesus' close friend John decided to write about his experiences with Jesus, he started out by calling Jesus the "Word of God." (see John 1) Think about that for a moment—Jesus is the word of God; He is the way God communicates with us!

When you have learned to read better, you will be able to read God's Word, the Bible, for yourself. Let's look at some of the words in God's book.

Letters and Sounds

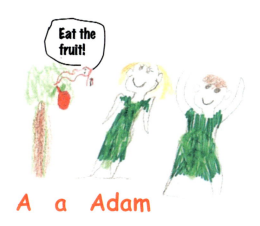

A   a   Adam

<u>A</u>dam <u>a</u>nd Eve were the first
people God made.
(see Genesis 3:20-21)

B   b   Bible

God's <u>b</u>ook, the <u>B</u>ible tells us
how God wants us to live.
(see 2 Timothy 3:16)

C   c   cross

Jesus was killed on a <u>c</u>ross.
(see John 19:16)

D   d   Daniel

<u>D</u>aniel was thrown into a <u>d</u>en
of lions. (see Daniel 6:16)

E e eagle

When we trust God, we will have **e**nergy and feel like flying as high as an **e**agle.
(see Isaiah 40:31)

F f forgive

We ask God to **f**orgive us, and we **f**orgive other people, too.
(see Matthew 6:9-12)

G g Goliath

David beat the **g**iant **G**oliath with a stone and a slingshot.
(see 1 Samuel 17:45)

H h help

God **h**elps us whenever we ask **H**im to.
(see Psalm 54:4)

I i I AM

God was in a burning bush when He told Moses, "**I** am who **I** am. That **is** my name: **I** AM." (see Exodus 3:14)

J j Jesus

We can **just** thank God for everything in **J**esus' name. (see Ephesians 5:20)

K k king

God is the **K**ing of **k**ings! (see 1 Timothy 6:15)

L l love

God wants us to **l**ove each other. (see 2 John 1:5)

M   m   manger

When Jesus was born, His **m**other put Him to bed in a **m**anger.
(see Luke 2:16)

N   n   Noah

Noah was a good man, and God saved his life in the flood.
(see Genesis 6:9)

O   o   open

God says He knocks **o**n the door **o**f **o**ur heart. He wants us to **o**pen the door and let Him in.
(see Revelation 3:20)

P   p   pray

Pray at all times.
(see 1 Thessalonians 5:17)

Q q
Queen
Esther

Queen Esther saved her people. (see Esther 5:3)

R r race

Life is like a race. We need to run the race and get a prize. (see 1 Corinthians 9:24)

I believe!

S s son

Martha said to Jesus, "I believe that You are the Son of God." (see John 11:27)

T t teach

Teach me about Your truth, Lord! (see Psalm 25:5)

U   u   understanding

We need to __u__nderstand how much God loves us!
(see Philippians 1:9)

V   v   vine

Jesus said He is like a __v__ine, and we are His branches. We need to be part of the __v__ine. (see John 15:5)

W   w   wall

Joshua and his men __w__alked around the __w__alls of Jericho just like God told them. And the __w__alls fell down!
(see Joshua 6:20)

X   x   eXtra

God wants us to share. If we have e__x__tra clothes or e__x__tra food, we should share it.
(see Luke 3:11)

Y y yes

and a wee little
man was he.

Z z Zaccheus

God doesn't want us to keep
saying, "I promise! I promise!"
He wants our "**Y**es" to mean
"**y**es." (see Matthew 5:37)

Zaccheus was too short to
see Jesus, so he climbed up
a tree. (see Luke 19:5)

Practice—
• Can you name the colored letters?
• Can you say or read the colored words?
• Can you find those words in the Bible verses?
• Find the letters in your name.
• Find the letters in God's name.
• What other words start with the letters?
• Can you tell any of the stories the verses and pictures are from?

Words with special jobs: colors

God made up all the colors there are! He painted the world with His beautiful colors. He made the leaves green. He made the flowers red and blue and purple and yellow and gold and pink and orange. He picked colors for the sunset, the sunrise, and the autumn leaves. He lovingly chose colors for skin, hair, and eyes.

And when God looked at all that He had made, He said,
"It is very good."
(see Genesis 1)

Then God shared His love for beauty with people. He chose some people to be artists and craftsmen. He chose these men and women to make beautiful things. They were put in charge of building God's house, where everyone would worship God (see Exodus 35).

After Noah's flood, God made the rainbow to tell us
He will never flood the whole world again. (see Genesis 9:8-17)

Practice—
• What colors do you see around you?
• What colors are in things God made?
• What's your favorite color? Why?
• What do you like to draw with? Make a colorful picture of something God
  made. Thank Him for making it!

Words with special jobs: rhymes

When God created language, He made special ways to use words. English, our language, uses rhyming words, like big/pig or funny/bunny. Can you hear the rhyming words in these Bible verses? If you have trouble, ask whoever is reading with you to tell one of the words that's in dark type and underlined. Then listen to the verse to find its rhyme. Ready?

The waters rose on the earth until all of the **<u>high</u>** mountains under the entire **<u>sky</u>** were covered. (Genesis 7:19)

The people will sing me a **<u>song</u>** all day **<u>long</u>**.
(see Lamentations 3:14)

When the queen of Sheba heard about the **<u>fame</u>** of Solomon and his relation to the **<u>name</u>** of the LORD, she came to test him with hard questions.
(1 Kings 10:1)

The soldiers who fought in the **<u>battle</u>** set apart as tribute for the LORD one out of every five hundred, whether persons, **<u>cattle</u>**, donkeys, sheep or goats. (Numbers 31:28)

Practice—
• Can you think of another rhyming word for some of these rhymes?
• Play a rhyming game. Pick a simple word, like <u>big</u> or <u>cat</u>. Say a rhyme for it.
  Another person says a different rhyme. Go around the group, sharing
  rhymes. Who is the last one to think of a rhyme?
• Can you find any words without rhymes? There are some!
• Here's a rhyming sentence: *I heard a bird.* Can you make up a rhyming
  sentence?

Words with special jobs: position

Some words tell us *where* something is, what its *position* is—is it **on** the table, **under** the table, or **in** the drawer? Listen for those words in these verses.

You made human beings the rulers **over** all that your hands have created. You put everything **under** their control. Psalm 8:6

He lets me lie down **in** fields of green grass. He leads me **beside** quiet waters. (Psalm 23:2)

I have put my rainbow **in** the clouds. It will be the sign of the covenant **between** me and the earth. Sometimes when I bring clouds **over** the earth, a rainbow will appear **in** them. Then I will remember my covenant **between** me and you and every kind of living thing. The waters will never become a flood to destroy all life again. (Genesis 9: 13-15)

Practice—

- Can you act out the position words? What would you do to show **over** in the first verse?
- Tell someone where something is. Use as many position words as you can. For example, you could ask for the book that is **on** the second shelf, **in** the bedroom, **next to** the door.
- Play a put-it-there game. Each person gives another directions, such as, "Put the rock **under** the table **by** the sofa **on** the yellow rug." You get a point for giving good directions, and a point for following the directions well.
- Notice position words when you're listening to a story or to someone talking.

Words with special jobs: opposites

It's fun to find words that mean the opposite of each other. Can you hear the opposite words in these verses?

Look at the ocean, so big and wide! It is filled with more creatures than people can count. It is filled with living things, from the **largest** to the **smallest**. (Psalm 104:25)

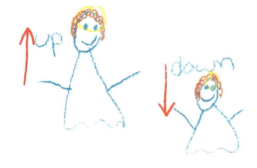

In a dream he saw a stairway standing on the earth. Its top reached to heaven. The angels of God were going **up** and coming **down** on it. (Genesis 28:12)

Be **joyful** with those who are joyful. Be **sad** with those who are sad. (Romans 12:15)

Don't drag me away with sinners. Don't drag me away with those who do evil. They speak in a **friendly** way to their neighbors. But their hearts are full of **hatred**. (Psalm 28:3)

But many who are **first** will be **last**. And many who are **last** will be **first**. (Matthew 19:30)

God rested from his **work**. Those who enjoy God's **rest** also **rest** from their **work**. (Hebrews 4:10)

I know what you are doing. I know you aren't **cold** or **hot**. I wish you were either one or the other! (Revelation 3:15)

Practice—
- Play the opposite game. For about 10 minutes, everyone has to say the opposite of what they are thinking. And you have to do the opposite of what someone tells you. For example, you could say, "Don't give me a cookie, please." And then you'd get a cookie! Of course, unless you're playing a game, it's not good to use opposites that way.
- Try this use of opposites. Whenever you say something negative or bad about someone or something, you have to say two opposite, good things. Like this, "I hate spinach. Um, spinach is a beautiful green, and Mom likes to cook it."

Writing in the Bible

God thinks writing is important! God writes, and He tells other people to write, too. We have the Bible because God told people to write down what He had been doing.

Dear children, I'm writing to you because your sins have been forgiven. They have been forgiven because of what Jesus has done. (1 John 2:12)

I am the Lord. I am the God of Israel. I say, "Write on a scroll all of the words I have spoken to you." (Jeremiah 30:2)

I, Paul, am writing this greeting with my own hand. (1 Corinthians 16:21)

Telling and listening to stories

It's both important and fun to understand stories. And it's good to be able to tell stories, too. Did you know God loves to tell stories? Listen to these verses ...

What I'm teaching also helps you understand proverbs and **stories**. It helps you understand the sayings and riddles of those who are wise. (Proverbs 1:6)

Jesus spoke all these things to the crowd by using **stories**. He did not say anything to them without telling a **story**. (Matthew 13:34)

Here's one of the stories Jesus told. (see Matthew 13:3-9)

A farmer was planting seed. Some of the seed fell on the path. Birds came and ate the seed. Some seeds fell where there was a little soil on rocks. The plants grew, but then they dried up in the sun. Other seeds were in thorns. The weeds kept the plants from growing well. But some of the seeds were on good soil. Those seeds grew into many strong plants! Jesus said the seed is people telling about Him. He said we are the soil. What kind of soil are you?

Practice:
- Every story has a beginning, a middle, and an end. And every story has a character (someone or something that the story's about). Most stories have a setting, too—the place the story happens.
- What happened at the beginning of this story?
- What happened in the middle?
- What happened at the end?
- Who was the story about?
- Where did the story happen?
- What would be a good title for this story?
- Can you answer those questions about a different story? How about the story about Jesus and the poor woman? It's in the part of the book about that talks about money.

Numbers and Math in the Bible

The Bible is full of numbers. God likes counting things, and He seems to like big, enormous numbers. Look at what He told Abraham about his children: God said Abraham would have one son. That son would have children, and they would have children, and *they* would have children. And all those people would tell other people about God. If the people believe in God, then they're Abraham's children, too!

God told Abraham he would have so many children, no one could count them. He said they would be more than the sand on the beach. He said they would be more than the stars in the sky. (see Genesis 15:5, 16:10, 32:12)

Counting

The Lord said to Samuel, "... I am sending you to Jesse in Bethlehem. I have chosen **one** of his sons to be king." 1 Samuel 16:1

1

God made **two** great lights. He made the larger light to rule over the day. He made the smaller light to rule over the night. (Genesis 1:16)

2

Then King Nebuchadnezzar leaped to his feet in amazement and asked his advisors, "Weren't there **three** men that we tied up and threw into the fire? ... Look! I see [them] walking around in the fire, unbound and unharmed!" (Daniel 3:22-23)

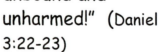

They were afraid we would crash against the rocks. So they dropped **four** anchors from the back of the ship. They prayed that daylight would come. (Acts 27:29)

Jesus took the **five** loaves and the two fish. He looked up to heaven and gave thanks. He broke them into pieces. Then he gave them to the disciples to set in front of the people. (Luke 9:16)

Six stone water jars stood nearby. ... Jesus said to the servants, "Fill the jars with water."
(John 2:6-7)

God told Noah, "Also take **seven** of every kind of bird. Take male and female of them. That will keep every kind alive. Then they can spread out again over the whole earth. (Genesis 7:3)

God was patient while Noah was building the ark. He waited, but only a few people went into the ark. A total of **eight** were saved by means of water. (1 Peter 3:20)

A mighty hero named Goliath came out of the Philistine camp. He was from Gath. He was more than **nine** feet tall. (1 Samuel 17:4)

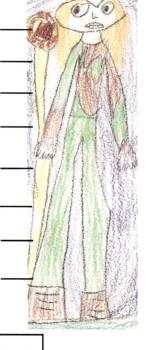

9

10

The Lord wrote on the tablets the words of the covenant. Those words are the **Ten** Commandments. (Exodus 34:28)

Then Peter stood up with the **Eleven**. In a loud voice he spoke to the crowd. "My Jewish friends," he said, "let me explain this to you." (Acts 2:14)

11

12

So Jesus appointed the **Twelve**:… Peter, James … and his brother John. … Andrew, Philip, Bartholomew, Matthew, Thomas, James … Thaddaeus, Simon [and] Judas. (Mark 3:16-18)
Jesus made his disciples get into the boat. He had them go on ahead of him. (Mark 6:45)

{1, 2, 3, 4, ... skip a few and count some more ... 20 ... and a hundred!}

The waters rose and covered the mountains to a depth of more than **twenty** feet. (Genesis 7:20)

20

Abraham was a **hundred** years old when his son Isaac was born to him. (Genesis 21:5)

100

Practice—
• How high can you count? Do it.
• How many people are in your family? How many adults? How many children? How many pets?
• How many chairs are in your house?
• How many books are in the bookshelf?
• How many trees are in your neighborhood?
• What else can you count?

Counting Blessings

What's something good that you have? That's a blessing from God! What's something good someone's done for you? That's a blessing from God, too!

Paul, who wrote most of the New Testament books in the Bible, says God gives us so many blessings, we can't count them all.

In 1897, a man named Johnson Oatman wrote a song. Here are the words to the chorus:

> Count your blessings, name them one by one,
> Count your blessings, see what God has done!
> Count your blessings, name them one by one,
> And it will surprise you what the Lord has done.

What are your blessings? Have someone write them down as you think of them. Pay attention as you go through the day. You'll find more and more blessings. Can you get as many as 100 blessings?

Here's the start of one child's list:
I love my cat.
I have new shoes, and they're green!
My mom makes good cookies.

$ ¢ Money ¢ $

Money seems very important to us. You ask for a toy or a candy bar, and Mother says, "We don't have enough money for that right now." Or maybe she asks, "Do you have enough money?" And then you have to count the coins in your bank or your pocket to see if you can buy it.

God knows how much we care about money. His Bible tells us two important things about money.

The first thing God wants us to know is that we can't buy anything from Him. What God wants us to have, He gives us for free.

One time, a man tried to buy God's power from Peter. Peter was really upset! Peter answered, "May your **money** be destroyed with you! Do you think you can buy God's gift with **money**?" (Acts 8:20)

Paul wrote many letters in the Bible about God's gift of eternal life. He said, "The **free** gift of God's grace makes all of us right with him. Christ Jesus paid the **price** to set us free." (Romans 3:24)

There's another thing God wants us to know about money. It's easy to think money is the most important thing there is, but that's not true. *God is more important than anything in our lives.*

Jesus said, "You can't serve God and **Money** at the same time." (Matthew 6:24)

And later the Bible says, "Don't be controlled by love for **money**. Be happy with what you have." (Hebrews 13:5)

Jesus knows that what's important isn't how much money we have. What's important is that we love Him.

One day, Jesus was watching some men and women bring money to the church to help the poor. He saw rich people giving large amounts of money. They knew their money would help lots of people.

Then Jesus saw a poor woman.
She put in two little coins that
were worth about 1¢ each.

Jesus was glad when He saw this.
He said to His disciples, "That poor
woman gave more than all those rich people!"

The disciples were surprised. They didn't understand how that could happen.

Jesus explained, "She gave even though she is poor. She put in everything she had. She gave all she had to live on." (see Mark 12:44)

Practice—
• What are the two big things God wants us to know about money?
• Do you have any money? What do you do with it?
• Do you ever give some of your money to help other people?
• Ask your family if they give money to help others. Can you help?

Do you know about money?

tails   heads

penny = 1¢
10 pennies=1 dime

nickel = 5¢

2 nickels = 1 dime

dime = 10¢
10 dimes = 1 dollar

quarter = 25¢
4 quarters = 1 dollar

$1

100 pennies = $1
20 nickels = $1
10 dimes   = $1
4 quarters = $1

Practice—

Look at some coins. What do you notice about them?

Maybe you saw that pennies are a different color (they're made of copper).

Maybe you noticed the pictures of people on the coins. Do you know who they are?

- Abraham Lincoln is on the penny. He freed the slaves.
- Thomas Jefferson is on the nickel. He wrote the Declaration of Independence.
- Franklin Roosevelt is on the dime. He helped our country at the start of World War II.
- George Washington is on the quarter. He was the first president.

Did you know blind people can tell what each coin is by feeling them?

This is how to do it:

Get the two bigger coins (the quarter and the nickel).

Feel the edges of those coins.

Did you feel the little lines around the edge of the quarter?

Now get the two littler coins (dime and penny).

Feel their edges.

The big quarter and the little dime both have rough edges.

The big nickel and the little penny both have smooth edges.

See if you can tell the coins apart by how they feel. Can your parents do it?

Hours, Days, and Months

People are always talking about time.
   "What time is it?"
   "How long till supper?"
   "When will the game be over?"
   "Wait till you're older."
   "What day is it?"
   "What's the date?"
   "Check the calendar!"

Sometimes we talk about time in big chunks: "It's the 21st century." (That's 100 years!) Sometimes we talk about time in middle-sized chunks: months and weeks. The bits of time we talk about get smaller and smaller: days, hours, minutes.

We know that God made everything. 'Way back at the beginning of everything, God created time. On the first day of creation, God made light and darkness. He called the light **day**, and He called the dark **night**. (see Genesis 1)

In God's Bible, people talk about minutes and hours. They talk about days and weeks, months and years. Time is very important to God.

Jesus Christ is the same **yesterday** and **today** and **forever**. (Hebrews 13:8)

Practice—
• Do you know the days of the week?
    Sunday, Monday, Tuesday, Wednesday, Thursday, Friday, Saturday
• How many days in a week? Count them.
• What day is today? What are you doing today?
• What day was yesterday? What did you do yesterday?
• What is tomorrow? What will you do tomorrow?
• What day do you go to church?
• What days do you go to school?

• Can you name the months in the year?
    January, February, March, April, May, June, July, August,
    September, October, November, December
• How many months are there? Count them.
• What month is this?
• What was last month?
• What's next month?
• What things happen in each month?
  Think about holidays, vacations,
  and other special things.

APRIL					
	1	2	3	4	5	6
7	8				

Seasons

[Ants] aren't very strong. But they store up their food in the **summer**. (Proverbs 30:25)

Look! The **winter** is past. The rains are over and gone. (Song of Songs 2:11)

People of Judah, ask the Lord to send rain in the **spring**. (Zechariah 10:1)

As they pass through the dry Valley of Baca, they make it a place where water flows. The rain in the **fall** covers it with pools. (Psalm 84:6)

May God be praised for ever and ever! ... He changes **times** and **seasons**. (Daniel 2:20-21)

Practice—
• What season is this?
• What happens at each season where you live?

SHAPES IN GOD'S WORLD

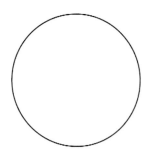

Then Jesus looked at the people sitting in a **circle** around him. (Mark 3:34)

The workers made an altar for burning incense. They made it out of acacia wood. It was one foot six inches **square** and three feet high. (Exodus 37:25)

My own hands spread out the heavens. I put all of the **stars** in their places. (Isaiah 45:12)

Jesus replied, "Love the Lord your God with all your **heart** and with all your soul. Love him with all your mind. (Matthew 22:37)

So you must go and make disciples of all nations. Baptize them in the name of the Father and of the Son and of the Holy Spirit.

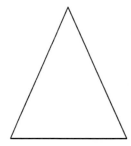

{Because the Trinity is three people, we can draw a triangle to show it.}
(Matthew 28:19)

Practice—
- We can think about shapes by how many sides they have (or, how many *angles* or points or corners they have).

    3 sides = triangle
    4 sides = square, rectangle
    5 sides = pentagon
    6 sides = hexagon (like a bee hive)
    8 sides = octagon (like a stop sign)

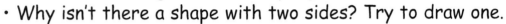

- Why isn't there a shape with two sides? Try to draw one.

- It's hard to find many of these shapes in God's creation. Can you guess why? Try this:
- Have someone cut a whole lot of squares, circles, and triangles from paper. Make a picture using just those shapes.
- How does your picture look? Does it look real? Why not?
- God is creative. He makes everything *unique*, which means there's nothing else exactly like it.

- There are also shapes that are 3-dimensional (3-D), so you can pick them up. Here are the names of some of those shapes:

    sphere (like a ball)
    cone (like an ice cream cone)
    cylinder (like a candle, or a drinking glass)
    cube (like a block)

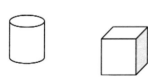

- What 3-D shapes can you find?

God made you! God knows you! God loves you!

Do you like to make things? Do you draw pictures, or build with clay or blocks? Do you make presents for your family?

If you've worked hard to make something beautiful or useful, you want other people to like it. You want them to take care of it.

God feels that way, too. He wants you to take care of your body, to keep it safe. And he wants you to respect other people's bodies, because He made them, too.

In the Bible, Paul wrote to some people about taking care of their bodies. He said, "Give yourselves to God. You have been brought from death to life. Give the parts of your body to him to do what is right." (Romans 6:13)

And then Paul said two amazing things.
He said, "Christ lives in you." (Romans 8:10)
And he said, "Don't you know that your
bodies are temples of the Holy Spirit?
The Spirit is in you. You have received him
from God. You do not belong to yourselves."
(1 Corinthians 6:19)

Wow! Jesus lives in us! God owns our bodies! We belong to Him!

Practice—
• How can you use your body to help other people?
• How can you use your body to help God?

God made your senses

When God created people, He wanted them to be able to enjoy His creation. So He made us so we can taste good food. We can smell wonderful smells. We can see beauty, and hear sounds. We can touch and feel things that are soft or smooth or slippery. God talks about your senses in His Bible.

Those who were blind could **see**. So the people praised the God of Israel. (Matthew 15:31)

Jesus **heard** that. So he said to them, "... I have not come to get those who think they are right with God to follow me. I have come to get sinners to follow me." (Mark 2:17)

But Jesus came and **touched** them. "Get up," he said. "Don't be afraid." (Matthew 17:7)

When Isaac smelled the clothes, he gave Jacob his blessing. He said, "It really is the **smell** of my son. It's like the smell of a field that the Lord has blessed." (Genesis 27:27)

Your words are very sweet to my **taste**! They are sweeter than honey to me. (Psalm 119:103)

Practice—
- What do you notice with your senses right now?
- Can you find a way to make someone else's senses happy? You could share a candy bar (taste and smell), or pat the cat (touch). What else can you think of to do?

God made your body

You placed a crown of pure gold on [the king's] **head**.
(Psalm 21:3)

Then Jesus began to wash his disciples' **feet**.
(John 13:5)

David wrote, "So my **heart** is glad. Joy is on my **tongue**. My **body** also will be full of hope.
(Acts 2:26)

The Lord would speak to Moses **face** to face. It was like a man speaking to his friend.
(Exodus 33:11)

You will hear your Teacher's voice behind you. You will hear it whether you turn to the **right** or the **left**. It will say, "Here is the path I want you to take. So walk on it." Isaiah 30:21

God knows all about you

God chose you because He loves you! He made you. He wants you to be just the way you are. And He wants you to learn to love Him and trust Him.

Brothers and sisters, we should always thank God for you. The Lord loves you. God chose you from the beginning. He wanted you to be saved. Salvation comes through the Holy Spirit's work. He makes people holy. It also comes through believing the truth.   (2 Thessalonians 2:13)

God has saved us. He has chosen us to live a holy life. It wasn't because of anything we have done. It was because of his own purpose and grace. Through Christ Jesus, God gave us that grace even before time began. (2 Timothy 1:9)

Practice—
• Ask someone to show you pictures of when you were born and when you were a little baby.
• Find out why your parents chose your name, and what they thought while they were waiting for you to be born.
• Thank God for loving you.
• Ask Him how you can be more like Him.

Lord, you have seen what is in my heart.
You know all about me.
(Psalm 139:1)

God knows your name.
The gatekeeper opens the gate for him. The sheep listen to his voice. He calls his own sheep by name and leads them out.
(John 10:3)   *Do you know your first and last name?*

God knows where you are.
But God understands the way to [wisdom]. He's the only one who knows where it lives.
(Job 28:23)   *Do you know your address?*

God calls to you.
Then Moses went up to God. The Lord called out to him from the mountain.
(Exodus 19:3)   *Do you know your phone number?*

God loves you.
God loved the world so much that he gave his one and only Son. Anyone who believes in him will not die but will have eternal life.
(John 3:16)   *Do you love God?*

Take a few minutes to talk to God now. Thank Him for making you. Thank Him for loving you. Tell Him anything else you want to. God always wants to hear about what you're thinking and feeling.

What the adult needs to know about teaching the skills

So keep my words in your hearts and minds. Write them down and tie them on your hands as a reminder. Also tie them on your foreheads. Teach them to your children. Talk about them when you are at home. Talk about them when you walk along the road. Speak about them when you go to bed. And speak about them when you get up. … So be careful. Obey all of the commands I'm giving you to follow. Love the Lord your God. Live exactly as he wants you to live. Remain true to him. (Deuteronomy 11:18-19, 22)

Teaching and learning these early skills should be fun for both you and your child. Feel free to use as much or as little detail as you want. Turn the activities into games; mention the skills as you drive or during a meal; genuinely praise your child as he or she begins to master the skills. This book offers several levels of instruction and interaction for you and your child:

- You can present the information as it is laid out here. Point to the letter A and tell your child its name and sound. Point to the picture and say, "A is for Adam!" Then move on.
- Elaborate on the story as much or as little as you like. After identifying A as the first letter of Adam, you can add something like, "Adam and Eve were the first people God made. They lived in God's garden and took care of the animals."
- Or, you can use the Scripture reference to tell the entire story, either in your own words or from the Bible. A children's Bible will probably be easier for your child to understand than your adult Bible. (We have used the New International Reader's Version.)
- Reading through the book at other times, you may want to ask questions: Do you remember this story? What letter is this? Can you find the letter R on this page?

Use the activities and questions at the end of each section as conversation starters and games to help your child continue to master and enjoy the skills.

What the adult needs to know about a Biblical Worldview

A Biblical worldview is what you believe about God and the Bible. It includes how well you live and try to live by what you believe. In other words, the person who believes spiders are helpful (but won't pick up a spider), or someone who believes statistics show air travel is safer than highway travel (but takes tranquilizers before a plane trip)—these people aren't living by their beliefs. Their "worldview" in these areas has no effect on their life.

A Biblical worldview answers the following basic questions:
- Who is God? Is He real? What is He like?
- What is the Bible? What does it tell us? Is it true?
- Who is Jesus? What did He do on earth? What does He do now?
- How and why was the world created? How should we treat creation?
- Why do bad things happen? Why do I make wrong choices?
- What is the nature and purpose of humanity? What does God want us to do?
- What happens after we die? Are heaven and hell real?
- What does God want us to do? What is salvation?
- What is truth? Is there a real truth, or is it different for different people?
- What spiritual authorities exist? How do we know what is right?

Here is one way to phrase the answers in child-friendly language:
God's in charge.
The Bible tells His story.
We are all sinners.
God made a plan to save us.
Jesus is the only way to be saved, to live with God forever.
The Bible tells us how to live.
This is the most important thing there is!

Thanks to the following members of the 2009 summer Sunday school class at Boulder Valley Christian Church, Boulder, Colorado, for their artistry and assistance:

Lila Butler, Reagan Christianssen, Matthew Coppanas, Carlee Cucksee, Sara Dias, Brennah Friesen, Cambria Green, Emma Harter, Lily Hefling, Shayna Hinz, Trevor James, Kade Jones, Makayla Jones, Kyle Leonesio, Bella Lopez, Henry Lopez, Kerry May Malone, Mike Malone, Max Manson, Mia Manson, Lily Morgan, Haley Morgan Patterson, Kali Reifsnyder, Tony Reifsnyder, Regan Reynolds, Riley Reynolds, Cole Schneider, Annabel Stewart, Abrey Taylor, Ashton Taylor, Nathan Totel, Natalie Treat, Angela Weddig, Walter Wesseling, and especially Michael Mote,

Thanks to the following for participating in photos:

From Truth Christian Academy (TruthChristian.com): Brienna Brace, Hyun Gyu Kim, Hyun Ook Kim, Inori Mori, Samuel Nixon, Nevaeh Ogden, Moriah Surdahl and Sierra Surdahl, and Mrs. Jessica Ogden

From Boulder Valley Christian Church (BVChristian.org): Chloe Bulpett, Julia Bulpett, Reagan Christianssen, Riley Christianssen, Kenny Cook, Croix Cope, Brennah Friesen, Ruthi Kingswood, Ryan Rosenblum, Courtney Webb, Taylor Webb, and Mrs. Mary Pilkington.

Our mission:

seeing children come to faith, one at a time,
guiding them to a Biblical worldview,
helping develop Godly character qualities, and
assisting parents in shepherding their children.

About the authors

Elsi Dodge is a single, retired teacher who works with a Chinese youth group, co-leads a women's Bible study, and advocates for families caught in the special education area of the public school system. In addition, she reads, sings, writes, and travels in a 30-foot RV, assisted by her Sallie, her beagle, and Dolphin, a saber-toothed tiger cleverly disguised as a tabby cat. She can be reached at ElsiDodge@aol.com or www.RVTourist.com/blog

Cathy Howe, a grandmother, is associate pastor of Boulder Valley Christian Church, Boulder, Colorado. She works with families facing difficult circumstances, supports orphans and children in foster care, and loves imparting a Biblical worldview to young people. She can be reached at Cathy@BVChristian.org